ASCD | arias

CO-PLANNING FOR FOR CO-TEACHING

Time-Saving Routines That Work in Inclusive Classroooms

D1571567

Gloria Lodato **WILSON**

ASCD

Alexandria, VA USA

Website: www.ascd.org   www.ascdarias.org
E-mail: books@ascd.org

Printed in the United States of America. ASCD publications present a variety of viewpoints. The views expressed or implied in this book should not be interpreted as official positions of the Association.

ASCD®, ASCD LEARN TEACH LEAD®, ASCD ARIAS® and ANSWERS YOU NEED FROM VOICES YOU TRUST® are trademarks owned by ASCD and may not be used without permission. All other referenced trademarks are the property of their respective owners.

PAPERBACK ISBN: 978-1-4166-2318-2   ASCD product #SF117018

Also available as an e-book (see Books in Print for the ISBNs).

Library of Congress Cataloging-in-Publication Data

Names: Wilson, Gloria Lodato, author.
Title: Co-planning for co-teaching : time-saving routines that work in
    inclusive classrooms / Gloria Lodato Wilson.
Description: Alexandria, Virginia : ASCD, [2016] | Includes bibliographical
    references.
Identifiers: LCCN 2016029773 (print) | LCCN 2016033018 (ebook) | ISBN
    9781416623182 (alk. paper) | ISBN 9781416623205 (PDF)
Subjects: LCSH: Teaching teams. | Teachers--Time management. | Inclusive
    education.
Classification: LCC LB1029.T4 W54 2016 (print) | LCC LB1029.T4 (ebook)
    | DDC

    371.14/8--dc23
LC record available at https://lccn.loc.gov/2016029773

24 23 22 21 20 19 18 17 16   1 2 3 4 5 6 7 8 9 10

ASCD | arias

CO-PLANNING FOR CO-TEACHING

Time-Saving Routines
That Work in Inclusive
Classrooms

Want to earn a free ASCD Arias e-book?
Your opinion counts! Please take 2–3 minutes to give
us your feedback on this publication. All survey
respondents will be entered into a drawing to
win an ASCD Arias e-book.

Please visit

www.ascd.org/ariasfeedback

Thank you!

Introduction

I love co-teaching but there is hardly any time for us to plan lessons. I'm in two elementary classes each day, a 2nd grade and 4th grade, so it is very difficult to co-plan with the two general education teachers. In addition, I've co-taught 2nd grade before but this is the first year that I am together with the 2nd grade teacher. I've never co-taught 4th grade so I am with a new co-teacher and learning a new curriculum.
–Special Education Co-Teacher, Elementary

I co-teach in 3 biology classes with 3 different general education teachers. Although the curriculum is pretty set, and I've made it my business to learn the content, the 3 teachers have very different styles. I'm able to co-plan with one co-teacher but not the others, so my role in each of the classes is very different. It's impossible to co-plan with 3 teachers.
–Special Education Co-Teacher, Secondary

Instituted to address diverse learning needs of students, inclusive classrooms wherein a general educator and special educator share the teaching duties—that is, co-teach—expanded and evolved throughout the past 20 years. Co-teaching in inclusive classrooms is commonplace in schools in the United States, and co-planning by co-teachers is both complex and time consuming. Often frustrated by lack of time for co-planning, co-teachers frequently over rely on ineffective ways of addressing the needs of students and become overwhelmed and discouraged.

Time-saving routines that both increase the active roles of each co-teacher and intensify instruction for students in inclusive settings make exponential differences in the learning of students. By co-thinking logistics, routines, strategies, and technologies, co-teachers streamline their co-planning and their co-teaching becomes more effective. This book provides co-teachers in inclusive settings, administrators supervising co-teachers, and pre-service teachers substantive suggestions and real-life examples on how co-teachers can co-plan effectively.

Co-Planning: The Key to Successful Co-Teaching

Why is co-planning so essential to successful co-teaching? Co-planning allows the general and special educators to communicate the needs of students in relation to the curriculum and the teaching of daily lessons and tasks. With co-planning, co-teachers realize together how the process of teaching content to students with exceptionalities requires focusing on the potential barriers that impede efficient learning. Co-planning allows co-teachers to find ways to remove the barriers to effective teaching practices while keeping the rigor of the coursework intact, to take the time to decide the big ideas that need to be understood and together make sure that those ideas are propelling lessons, and to create learning environments that support all learners and enable students to succeed. With co-planning, parity between the co-teachers is entrenched in spirit and in reality.

Without co-planning, lessons often remain unchanged, and the needs of diverse learners may not be specifically addressed. Without co-planning, parity between the co-teachers can be illusive and may result in one co-teacher doing the bulk of the planning and teaching. Without co-planning, students with special needs are likely to be under-served and their needs only marginally met.

Making the most of two teachers in an inclusive class-room is intricately aligned to the level of co-planning and an understanding of the appropriateness of each of the five major models of co-teaching routinely incorporated within daily classroom lessons.

Five Co-Teaching Models

Effective co-planning requires an understanding of the five major co-teaching models—one teach/one support; team-ing; alternative; parallel; and station. Each model has its place in a co-taught inclusive classroom (Wilson & Blednick, 2011). Co-teachers who analyze and reflect on the models they commonly employ, and who make adjustments to intensify instruction and deepen learning, understand their paired teaching potential. After reflection, co-teachers who are willing to alter their typical practices, which may be more comfortable though not maximally effective, often realize that they can teach more in less time—and that students learn more.

One Teach/One Support

This model of co-teaching, wherein one teacher is primarily responsible for the planning and execution of the lessons while the other co-teacher offers roaming support to students, occasionally interjecting points and assessing student learning, requires very little, if any, co-planning. The one teach/one support model is pervasive in co-taught classes due, in part, to the belief that the roaming teacher is indeed giving students the individual attention needed by noticing confusion and clarifying points. Both co-teachers are actively involved in teaching the students.

However, this "butterfly approach," where one co-teacher briefly interacts with a number of students, is less effective than other co-teaching models in delivering the degree of support needed for diverse learners, can lead to disparate roll identification and workload, and generally undermines the vision of an inclusive classroom where co-teachers deliver intensive instruction to all students. Quantifying the frequency of the use of the one teach/one support model enlightens co-teachers' practice and compels co-teachers to seek other models. If co-teachers find they are using the one teach/one support model the majority of the time, they need to reflect, redirect, and try a co-teaching model that lowers the ratio of students to teachers and enables co-teachers to better assess learning, adjust instruction, and give more students opportunities to respond.

Teaming

In the teaming model, co-teachers teach to the entire class and together offer information and comments. Often this becomes a "ping-pong" method, where co-teachers take turns delivering instruction and supporting students. One co-teacher can take one point of view, the other another; one co-teacher can deliver content while the other highlights strategies that students must understand and remember. As it turns out, many co-teachers who believe that they are using the teaming model are actually using the one teach/ one support model.

While this model creates parity of roles with the co-teachers and the students, it does little to increase student responses or differentiate instruction, is less effective than models that result in better student to teacher ratios, affords students few opportunities to respond, and doesn't allow co-teachers to fully assess student performance or adapt instruction.

Alternative

This co-teaching model is often employed when co-teachers feel that the skill level of a select number of students is far below that of their classmates. Often called the "back-table" model, in alternative co-teaching, one co-teacher takes a small group of students (usually those who are having some difficulties) to a separate part of the room—often the back table. This co-teacher pre-teaches, re-teaches, and practices with the small group the prerequisite and requisite skills for the content being delivered by the other co-teacher, who teaches the majority of the students.

While the "back-table" application of the alternative model is at times needed, its overuse creates a virtual "other" class—or a class within a class—and leads to stigmatization of the students grouped in this way. Rather than decreasing skill disparities, this model can actually increase the achievement gap by holding up the progression of learning and limiting the scope of the curriculum.

Parallel

When initially introduced to parallel co-teaching—the splitting of the class into two heterogeneous groups with each co-teacher delivering instruction to a group—co-teachers usually protest. Typical objections are that it's distracting to students and co-teachers, or that the classrooms are not large enough to accommodate two simultaneous lessons. But after visiting thousands of co-taught classes and seeing the parallel model in action, I can attest to the fact that after a period of adjustment, modifying teacher voice volume, rearranging desks, and customizing content, co-teachers see the power of this model. This model offers students an opportunity to focus more closely on the lesson and participate more fully, and co-teachers an opportunity to assess student learning, adjust teaching accordingly, and target learning.

Parallel co-teaching can take a number of forms. One way is for both teachers to teach identical content. Another is for each teacher to teach a component of a lesson to a group of students and then have the groups switch so that every student receives all of the content—making it a virtual two-station model. While the student groups are usually heterogeneous, students may at times be grouped homogeneously, according to need.

Station

Station co-teaching, not to be confused with cooperative learning groups, requires the division of the class into three or four heterogeneous groupings that rotate throughout the class period. Two of the stations are directly taught by the co-teachers, and the remaining one or two stations are independent stations. In the teacher-directed stations, co-teachers actively interact with students who are engaged in lessons that require investigation of topics, teacher modeling, guided practice, and thoughtful discussions. In these small-group teacher-directed stations, teachers can customize the delivery of the lesson as they are continually provided with opportunities to assess student learning, enlightenment, or confusion. In the independent stations, students can work alone or interact with others on a particular task.

With the station model, each station, although addressing various aspects of a topic, must stand on its own. What is learned in one station is not dependent on any other station since in a three-station lesson, each student group starts at a different station.

The creation of the independent stations takes some practice—as the students must complete the task during the allotted station rotation time, and the material must be at a level that will enable students to complete the activity without the assistance of a teacher. The tasks must also engage students sufficiently so that they will remain focused without teacher support.

Finding the Right Mix: Which Models Work Best Together

Once teachers understand the different co-teaching models, co-teachers' reflection on their current practices can lead to substantive changes. By discussing the different co-teaching models and assessing each in relation to the percentage of time that a given model is used during the co-teachers' time together, and under which circumstances, co-teachers can determine the extent to which they must adjust their practices to better serve their students.

The table in Figure 1 may be expanded as needed to keep track of a week's worth of co-teaching sessions. After reviewing a week, co-teachers co-analyze the tasks and their corresponding co-teaching models, the efficacy of the tasks/lessons, and what changes might be needed.

FIGURE 1: **Co-Teaching Session Log**

Date:	Time:	Task:	TT	Tt	P	S	A	Notations

TT = Teaming   Tt= One teach/one support   P=Parallel   S=Station   A=Alternative

For each model, co-teachers can answer the following questions:

- For what percentage of time do we use the _____ model?
- For which lessons or tasks do we routinely use this model?
- What are the advantages of using this model with this routine?
- What are the disadvantages of using this model routinely?
- How well do students learn when we use this model?
- Is there another model we should try for this routine that is more beneficial for student learning?
- What co-planning do we need to do if we decide to use a different model for this particular routine?
- What roles will each of us play in this adjusted routine?

Co-Plan Logistics

Devising a Co-Planning Schedule

For effective co-planning, it is essential that co-teachers meet other than during actual class time. Co-teachers need to set aside time for co-planning—whether or not the time is administratively woven into their day. Admittedly, this is a challenge, but all teachers spend time outside of the school day planning, creating materials, and marking papers. While co-teachers must spend time co-planning outside of the school day, the amount of time needed can be minimized and the time spent optimized if the co-teachers first focus on logistics such as the coordination of schedules.

Co-teachers can devise optimal co-planning times by answering the following questions:

- What time do each of us typically arrive in the morning? Leave the school at day's end?
- When do we each have administrative duty periods? Planning periods?
- What time during the school day do we have mutual free time to co-plan?
- When during the evening is a good time to occasionally call to discuss plans?
- How often do each of us check texts and e-mails?
- Are there any times or days when keeping in contact is off limits?

Setting Up the Co-Taught Classroom

Arranging furniture impacts the ease of co-teaching. The thoughtful arrangement of classroom furniture facilitates parallel and station teaching by creating spaces through which students and teachers can fluidly move. Frequently, co-teachers who wish to employ the parallel and station co-teaching models state that lack of classroom space, or the time involved in getting students into two or more groups, creates barriers to actual implementation. By thoughtfully considering the desk placements for both teachers and students, co-teachers may be surprised at how easy it is to form groups and organize lessons.

Co-Teachers' Desks. An often overlooked space guzzler is a teacher's desk; multiply that by two and a great deal of the classroom space is consumed. *But how can there not be teachers' desks in the classroom, and doesn't co-teacher parity require that each co-teacher have a desk?* If the classroom used for co-teaching is not shared with other teachers, co-teachers can find space-saving alternatives by answering the following questions:

- How much time do we sit at our desks and work during the day? Before and after school?
- Does the desk serve as a computer station?
- Is the desk used as a table for lesson plans, materials, staplers, tape?
- What is contained in the drawers? How often are the contents used?
- What files are stored in the file drawer? How often are the files accessed?
- Are there alternative spaces within the classroom for the computer, supplies, files, materials?

Once co-teachers analyze the use of their desks, they can usually find alternate locations for items stored on or in the desk (e.g., a vertical file cabinet, a rolling stack of drawers for supplies, a windowsill with dividers for storing handouts, a small table and chair to facilitate computer use).

Students' Desks. Rearranging students' desks based on an analysis of their placement and use can also free up space and facilitate groupings. It would be helpful to consider the following questions when arranging the classroom for co-teaching:

- Are there any students who have "preferential seating" on their Individualized Educational Program (IEP)?
- How do we define "preferential seating"?
- How can we arrange seating so that co-teachers can easily move around the room?
- How can we group students so that no student feels stigmatized?
- How can we arrange seating to maximize individual instruction?
- How can we arrange furniture to facilitate grouping with minimal disruption?
- How can we arrange the desks so that all students can easily view the interactive or main whiteboard?
- Do we have tables for student groupings? Are tables preferable to desks?
- How does desk grouping affect student behavior?
- What is the maximum group size that we will need?

For more information on effective room arrangement, go to https://iris.peabody.vanderbilt.edu/wp-content/uploads/pdf_case_studies/ics_effrmarr.pdf.

Elementary school desk set-up examples. One of the most beneficial desk configurations in an elementary classroom is clusters of desks in squared-off U-shaped configurations. For example, in a class with 30 desks, three groups of 10 desks can be arranged by placing four desks at the bottom of the U and three desks at each side of the U, as shown on the left side of Figure 2. A chair may be placed in the center, and co-teachers can easily and effortlessly access every student.

Another configuration that co-teachers might consider is opposing E-shaped clusters, as shown on the right side of Figure 2. The 30 student desks are divided into two opposing E-shaped clusters with six desks forming the vertical portion of the E and three desks forming each of the horizontal portions of the E. With this desk configuration, each E-shaped cluster can be used for parallel co-teaching, and the sections within each E effectively facilitate station co-teaching.

FIGURE 2: **U-Shaped Desk Configurations**

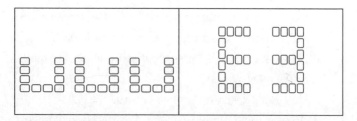

Secondary school desk set-up examples. Middle and high school classrooms are often shared spaces, with multiple teachers using the rooms throughout the day. This creates somewhat of an obstacle for co-teachers who want to arrange the desks to facilitate groupings. In any case, considering alternative arrangements to traditional desks in rows can prove to be quite beneficial to co-teaching models. Some configurations to consider include:

- Traditional rows with an aisle down the center (see upper right hand of Figure 3)
- Two facing rows of desks
- Angled rows on the left and right sides of the classroom, and straight rows in the center (see upper left hand of Figure 3)
- Three vertical clusters of desks (see lower right hand of Figure 3)
- Desks in L/reverse L configurations

FIGURE 3: **Desk Set-Up Configurations**

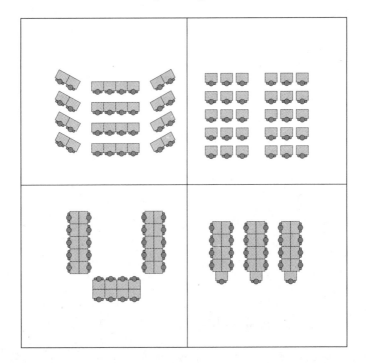

Co-Plan Routines

Examining daily routines and establishing roles, responsibilities, and co-teaching models increases efficient co-planning. No matter how good the intentions of the co-teachers, co-planning every aspect of every lesson is daunting—if not impossible. By concentrating on the class elements that are routine, and then identifying ways to make the co-teaching of these elements routine, co-teachers minimize the amount of co-planning that is needed and maximize the effectiveness and efficiency of their partnership (Wilson, 2015). By answering the following questions, co-teachers can identify and examine often-employed routines:

- What practices or tasks do we routinely use during co-teaching?
- How do we begin the co-teaching period? Are there particular morning routines?
- Does the period start with a warm-up or a Do Now?
- Does the period end with an exit question or other type of assessment?
- How often is the interactive whiteboard used, and for how long?
- How is a unit introduced?
- How are tasks and skills modeled? Is guided practice regularly employed? How do students use class time for independent practice?

- Is homework assigned daily or are homework packets used? When and how is homework checked?
- Are quizzes given regularly? Is there typically a test at the end of a unit? What do quiz and test reviews look like? Do test reviews take place within the class? Are test review packets given to students? When?
- How are special projects organized?

After addressing the questions above and listing their class routines, co-teachers then identify a routine to analyze. In analyzing a routine, co-teachers consider the following:

- What model of co-teaching do we currently employ during this routine?
- Is one co-teacher primarily responsible for the content of this routine?
- How much opportunity is there during this routine to assess student performance? To adapt materials or instruction?
- How much opportunity is there during this routine for students to respond? To get individualized attention?
- How are students performing during this routine? Do some students benefit more than others?

Then, in deciding how to revise the routine to make the most of the time devoted to it, co-teachers must consider the following:

- Which co-teaching model will lead to more intensive instruction during this routine?
- Which model will increase student learning?

- Which model will allow for more assessment of learning?
- Which model will allow for more opportunities for student responses?
- Which model will provide occasions to adjust instruction and adapt materials?

Re-Worked Routines

Elementary School Examples

Routine: Morning Work. 5th grade co-teachers review their 20-minute morning work routine.

Current routine. Weekly morning work packets include spelling word practice, vocabulary exercises, a free-writing prompt, a sampling of math word problems, and a short reading passage with questions. All students are given identical packets. Students complete the packets independently during the first 20 minutes of each day while co-teachers take attendance, review parent notes, collect homework, and supervise students.

Co-teachers' reflection on the routine. The co-teachers like this routine because it allows time for students to enter the room, get settled, and begin work. It also provides co-teachers with time to take care of some necessary procedural work.

However, while some of the students complete the work quickly, others barely make a dent in the packet. There is rarely time to provide assistance to the students who need it.

Adjusted routine. The co-teachers realize that, at the very least, the work packets need to be differentiated to the students' independent skill levels. They look at the completed work packets and analyze student progress and errors. The co-teachers create three work packets with varying levels of difficulty for subjects included in the work packets—spelling, vocabulary, writing, word problems, and reading passages—and collate weekly packets according to students' skill levels in each of the areas. Students are then given differentiated individualized packets with the appropriate skill level for each area. For example, a student with a high skill level in spelling, vocabulary, writing, and reading passages and low skill level in math word problems will be given a work packet that corresponds to his or her skill levels.

The co-teachers also decide that, in addition to creating differentiated packets, they will try an alternative co-teaching model whereby one co-teacher will take attendance, read parent notes, check homework, and supervise students while the other co-teacher will work closely with a different group of three to four students each day. In the small group setting, the co-teacher will review the students' progress on their morning work, discuss goals and improvement, and further customize student packets. Co-teachers will switch roles weekly so that each will be able to work closely with small groups of students.

Benefits of the adjusted routine. Customizing the weekly packets to correspond to students' skill levels maximizes the benefits of the time spent on the activities each day. Use of the alternative co-teaching model allows the co-teachers to carefully assess student work, and to discuss with the students their accomplishments and targeted areas of need. Strategies can be developed, and intensive and directed instruction facilitated.

Routine: Reading Block. 2nd grade co-teachers review their reading block.

Current routine. The first 45 minutes is devoted to the foundations of decoding, and the students are broken into guided reading groups for the remaining 45 minutes. The co-teachers employ the teaming co-teaching model for the first half of the reading block. The co-teachers take turns presenting the mini-lessons on the phonetic and structural elements of reading to the entire class, and afterwards both teachers circulate to determine whether the students understand the tasks. If students are having difficulties with the tasks, either co-teacher sits next to the student and offers support.

During the guided reading section of the reading block, the second 45 minutes of the block, the students are placed in leveled groupings and the co-teachers each have assigned groups that they prepare for and work with.

Co-teachers' reflection on the routine. The co-teachers know that there is a wide variance in students' abilities in the phonetic and word analysis lessons; some students have no difficulties and others only minimally acquire the important elements. Therefore, the lessons seem too simple for some and too difficult for others. Routine assessments show that students who are weak in decoding are making only marginal progress. The pacing is simultaneously too fast and too slow. The co-teachers realize that they are "pulling some of the needier students along" in order to keep up with the pacing schedule set by the district, and that more concentrated instruction is required for some of the students.

The co-teachers are satisfied with the guided reading portion of their reading block and feel that students are given the attention needed and that the work of students in all groups has improved.

Adjusted routine. The co-teachers considered the alternative co-teaching model, but felt that it might stigmatize the students and slow the progression of skills introduced. They decide to try the station model first. They divide their 30 students into three heterogeneous groups of 10. They also divide their foundations of decoding program into a phonetic component and word structure component; each will be a station with each co-teacher responsible for one of the two components. Together they plan for the independent group/station and create a variety of phonetic and word structure games with self-correction components. Each day, each group spends 15 minutes at each station. The 45-minute guided reading segment of the reading block is unchanged.

Benefits of the adjusted routine. The pacing of the reading components remains intact, but the smaller groupings allow the teachers to assess student performance and adjust the materials to meet the needs of the 10 students in each group. If some students need additional support, the co-teachers can continue use of the station model for three or four days a week and change to the alternative model with a homogeneous small group for one or two days.

Routine: Read Aloud. 1st grade co-teachers review the 20-minute read aloud.

Current routine. All students sit on the rug while one co-teacher, sitting on a chair, reads and displays the book to the class and discusses characters, plot development, and literary elements. The other co-teacher sits on the rug and positions herself near students who tend to be distracted or restless. Both co-teachers ask students questions and highlight important information. Students periodically pair with partners to discuss an element of the book. While the co-teachers feel that they are employing the teaming model, the format more closely resembles the one teach/one support model.

Co-teachers' reflection on the routine. The co-teachers feel that it is very important for the students to meet as an entire class to learn to listen attentively for a period of time and to interact with one another. However, after reviewing the routine for a few days, they realize that a limited number (usually the same students) are answering questions. They also notice that during student partnering, the students with limited skills usually partner with each other (since they are sitting in close proximity to the co-teacher on the rug) and that the students who are restless continue to fidget.

Adjusted routine. The co-teachers decide that they want more students to participate and want the partnerings to be more strategic. They decide to mix up story time a bit and alternate between the co-teaching model they now use—one teach/one support—and the parallel model. When the entire class is on the rug, the students are situated so that the skill levels of partners are more varied. The co-teachers arrange for students to have different partners each day of the week. The co-teachers also intermittently use popsicle sticks with students' names to pick students to answer questions.

Every other day, the co-teachers employ the parallel model and divide the students into two heterogeneous groups and position the groups on opposite sides of the room. Each group, led by a co-teacher, is either read the same book or books with similar themes. If time permits, after the book is read and discussed, the entire class comes together, with students paired one from each group to share their understanding of the books read to them.

Benefits of the adjusted routine. The co-teachers reach a compromise between whole class (one teach/one support) and half class (parallel) instruction. They address the challenges of the whole group story reading by breaking up the class into two groups. In this way, more students can participate and focus on the story, and the benefits of whole-group story reading remain as the whole class is read to on alternate days. The co-teachers realize that adjusting the routine does not leave them with an all-or-nothing approach.

Routine: Math Word Problems. 4th grade co-teachers review how they teach students to solve word problems.

Current routine. The co-teachers allocate 30 minutes three times a week solely for the purpose of teaching strategies for solving math word problems. The interactive whiteboard is used for this activity and students are taught as one group. One co-teacher always takes the lead and the other supports students as needed.

Co-teachers' reflection on the routine. The co-teachers believe that word problems are an important component of their math curriculum and that students benefit from the close deconstruction of the word problems. The co-teacher leading the whole group uses a "thinking out loud" meta-cognitive strategy demonstrating the methodical manner of thinking about and solving word problems. The co-teachers really like the richness of the lessons with which the interactive whiteboard is used, and highlight (in color) words and information, manipulate images, and prompt students to interact with the words, symbols, and pictures. The direct teaching and interaction with students is very important and the co-teachers are beginning to see that many of the students are successfully solving word problems independently.

However, the co-teachers are a bit frustrated by the wide divergence of reading and arithmetic abilities of the students, as well as the glaringly obvious need of some students for extensive modeling and guided practice in math word problem techniques. They also notice that allocating 30 minutes to solve one or two problems causes students, initially attentive, to become restless.

Adjusted routine. The co-teachers decide to use the parallel model of co-teaching, first with heterogeneous groups and then with homogeneous groups. They both teach the same math story to half of the class. Use of the interactive whiteboard becomes a bit problematic: both teachers want to use it as it's particularly useful with word problems. The teachers decide that one will use the interactive whiteboard and the other a presentation pad. As word problems are done three times a week, the teachers will alternately use the interactive whiteboard.

After each heterogeneous group solves math word problems for 15 minutes, the class is regrouped into two homogeneous groups according to skill level. One co-teacher leads the group that needs more intensive guided practice. The other co-teacher closely assesses and assists the group that is more proficient in word problems, and whose members are given advanced word problems to solve in pairs or independently.

Benefits of the adjusted routine. More students respond to questions, the students are generally more attentive, and teachers can assess and respond to students and adjust materials as needed. The homogeneous skill groups enable the students to both receive the reinforcement or advancement needed while being exposed to the expected level of curriculum.

Secondary School Examples

Routine: Review for Unit Tests. 9th grade English students are given study guides to complete.

Current routine. The students are given a study guide two days before their unit test to complete for homework. The day before the unit test, a Jeopardy game is displayed on the interactive whiteboard and students are put into heterogeneous teams and take turns answering the Jeopardy game prompts. The co-teachers take turns revealing the questions and discussing the answers.

Co-teachers' reflection on the routine. After checking the students' study guides, the co-teachers realize that some students complete the study review sheets better than others —as expected. When they discuss the guides with the students, they discover that some students spend an inordinate amount of time completing them, some do them quickly but inaccurately, and few are actually using them to study. During the Jeopardy game, the students who know the questions to the answers respond for their groups—and only a select few respond. While the students seem to enjoy the activity, the co-teachers are not sure if enough actual review and learning takes place. Some students, despite the study guides and the review game, continue to score poorly on unit tests.

Although both co-teachers are involved, there is little individualization or intensity of instruction, and co-teachers want to devise a review that goes deeper into the concepts and issues of the unit and involves all students.

Adjusted routine. The co-teachers decide to give students the study guides at the beginning of the unit and students complete the guides as the unit develops through Do Nows, homework assignments, and exit tickets. During the review session the day before the test, the class is split into four heterogeneous groups; two are teacher-directed stations and two are independent stations. Students switch stations every 10 minutes.

One independent group uses a deck of cards divided into questions and answers and matches the questions with the correct answers. The other independent group plays the Jeopardy game on the interactive whiteboard; an emcee and score keeper are named and run this station. In the teacher-directed stations, one co-teacher discusses the more complex concepts of the unit with one group while the other co-teacher practices multiple choice and essay questions, providing strategies for test taking, with the other group.

Benefits of the adjusted routine. Completing the study guides as the unit develops gives a continuity to the lessons and enables co-teachers to assess student understanding throughout the unit. The review class made up of four stations before the exam supports deep student learning and student participation, and gives the co-teachers the opportunity to target concepts that need clarification.

Routine: Introduction of New Material. 7th grade Social Studies students are presented with new material via an interactive whiteboard.

Current routine. The new topic is presented through a PowerPoint presentation and students follow along with note sheets, responding to questions posed by the co-teacher leading the presentation. The other co-teacher moves around the room and assists various students, making sure that students are on task.

Co-teachers' reflection on the routine. The co-teachers like the flexibility of the PowerPoint presentation and insert videos, pictures, and questions. While many of the students pay attention and seem engaged, some of the students need to be redirected. As very few students respond to the questions posed, the co-teachers are not sure how much the students remember from the PowerPoint presentation—during which the students with special needs are the most passive. The supporting co-teacher keeps the students on track, but has a limited role.

Adjusted routine. The co-teachers decide that the Power-Point presentations are important and want to elicit more student interaction. They decide to try the parallel co-teaching model and teach two different aspects of a topic. They divide the students into two heterogeneous groups that switch between co-teachers in 20 minutes. One co-teacher presents a topic to one group via PowerPoint. The other co-teacher leads one group in a discussion of the topic, discovers what the students know about the topic (or what the group who viewed the PowerPoint presentation learned from it), and introduces new vocabulary words.

Benefits of the adjusted routine. By limiting the PowerPoint presentation to 20 minutes, students remain attentive. By grouping students, students have more opportunities to respond to and ask questions, and co-teachers can better assess student knowledge and understanding and clarify vocabulary and concepts.

Routine: Beginning of Class. 8th grade Math students display their homework on their desks as they complete a Do Now worksheet.

Current routine. As the students complete the Do Now worksheet independently, one co-teacher circulates around the room and the other co-teacher takes attendance and then checks homework. After approximately five minutes, one co-teacher goes over the Do Now worksheet with the entire class. Afterwards, the other co-teacher takes over and reviews the math problems assigned for homework that many students found difficult. Total time allocated is approximately 12 minutes.

Co-teachers' reflection on the routine. The co-teachers like this established routine because students get settled and start working quickly on an activity whereby something learned is reviewed or students begin to think about the upcoming lesson. Homework check and attendance procedures are quickly accomplished and both teachers are actively involved.

The co-teachers note that it takes some students quite a bit of time to put away their books and start working. In fact, three or four students rarely finish the Do Now worksheet, and most students do not participate in the discussion that follows its completion. Although the co-teachers allocate 12 minutes to the Do Now and homework check, they find that they actually take 20 minutes—particularly if they need to re-teach some of the homework concepts. As well, the co-teachers are dissatisfied with students' performance on quizzes and unit exams.

Adjusted routine. The co-teachers decide to adhere to their current routine for three days of the week and change the routine two days a week, employing a different review strategy each of the two days. One review strategy involves a Quick Review. Using a PowerPoint, co-teachers create a series of the 10 most important short questions for each unit that is taught. Each question is on a separate slide, all slides within a unit have the same background color (e.g., all slides with questions regarding multiplication with exponents are red, and slides with questions regarding the polynomial unit are blue), and the slides are randomized. (Alternatively, questions can be written on colored construction paper.) One day a week, for eight minutes at the beginning of class, one co-teacher presents questions as students respond individually on whiteboards. The other co-teacher takes attendance and checks homework.

Another review strategy incorporates a peer tutoring activity. For an activity that focuses primarily on vocabulary, students are paired and one is designated the tutor and the other the tutee. The tutors are given a peer tutoring sheet with two columns. The first column consists of 10 questions that pertain to the current unit. The second column consists of single-word answers (the only type supplied, for answer clarity) to the questions in the first column. The third column is for scoring: students who answer correctly on the first try receive a score of 2; a correct answer on the second try is scored as a 1; and students who fail to answer the question correctly twice receive a score of 0. If time permits, the tutee becomes the tutor. One co-teacher supervises the peer tutoring while the other co-teacher takes attendance and checks homework.

Benefits of the adjusted routine. By keeping the Do Now and homework routine for three days a week and instituting the two review strategies, the co-teachers realize that they can accomplish multiple goals. They incorporate review strategies that are quick and cumulative and that give students multiple, low-stakes opportunities during a unit to learn.

Routine: Science Lab. 10th grade Science class students attend bi-weekly lab sessions that include lab stations and lab sheets.

Current routine. One co-teacher leads the class and describes and demonstrates the lab activity. Students are paired according to skill level and are expected to complete the experiment and answer the questions on the lab sheet.

The co-teacher who led the lab activity circulates around the lab stations and supervises student activity. The other co-teacher works directly with the three pairs of students who have the most difficulty reading, following directions, and completing the labs independently.

Co-teachers' reflection on the routine. The co-teachers reflect on the lab activities. They realize that the initial explanations and demonstrations take approximately 15 minutes of the 45-minute period and, as many students do not pay close attention during this time, numerous questions arise as students complete the lab and attempt to answer the questions. The co-teachers also closely review the completed lab packets and notice that most student pairs write exactly the same answers. As a result, the co-teachers are not sure how much learning is taking place. The pairs of students who are more closely supervised by one of the co-teachers rely heavily on the co-teacher to guide them through the experiments and to complete the lab packet questions; these students receive low grades, as their lab packets are usually incomplete.

The co-teachers decide to test their students' knowledge of the experiments and create a short lab test, given the day after the lab. Many of the students do poorly, particularly the students with the weakest skills. The co-teachers realize that the explanation and demo of the lab and actual implementation of the lab are not sufficient for lasting student learning, and co-teachers wonder how deep the learning is from the lab experiences. However, the co-teachers feel that their use of the alternative co-teaching model for lab experiments holds some promise and want to continue using the model. They look into how they are supporting students' lab practice.

Adjusted routine. During the demonstration and modeling portion of the experiment, the co-teachers display on the whiteboard a Lab Steps Chart that clearly delineates the progression of the particular lab. The Lab Steps Chart, the first page of the lab packet, includes a step-by-step how-to for the lab, with check-off boxes for each step. The co-teachers keep the required elements for all of the labs, but change the format, scaffold some of the material, and devise various ways for students to respond to the questions as needed. Question responses are in the form of fill-ins, drawings, or answering multiple choice or open-ended questions.

The co-teachers also include an additional self-monitoring tool in the packet—annotation bubbles and Watch Out statements—at points where students often encounter difficulties. The annotation bubbles consist of short questions asking if the students included an important element in their response; Watch Out statements caution students to be on the lookout for a tricky section. The co-teachers also include in the packet an evaluation sheet that asks students to rate their understanding of the lab.

Benefits of the adjusted routine. The co-teachers retain the original—alternative—co-teaching model and consider other ways to customize and intensify instruction. By carefully reviewing the lab packets and adjusting the format of the packets (e.g., including various answer formats, annotation bubbles, and Watch Out statements) while maintaining their rigor, students are closely guided through the activities.

Addressing Students' Needs in the Co-Taught Classroom

Incorporating and routinely implementing core strategies into co-planning addresses students' Individualized Educational Program (IEP) goals and maximizes the impact of lessons. Students with special needs have IEPs—documents that delineate individual students' educational goals to be addressed in the most appropriate setting. (For more information, go to https://www .understood.org/en/school-learning/special-services/ieps /understanding-individualized-education-programs.)

When the co-taught inclusive setting is chosen, the IEP goals must be addressed. Therefore, in addition to curriculum goals for all students in an inclusive classroom, the IEP goals for students with special needs must also be a focus. Co-teachers may at times feel that the IEP goals and grade level curriculum goals are at odds with each other, with maximum focus on the rising curriculum demands and little time to concentrate on IEP goals. However, in recent years, IEP goals have been more closely aligned to curriculum goals, making the link between the two easier to address. IEP goals are actually the bridge between students' present levels of performance and general education expectations and the means to rise to curriculum goals (see http://www .lease-sped.org/files/Teachers/Aligning_CCSS.pdf).

Both IEP and curriculum goals will be difficult to meet if co-teachers approach their inclusive class as a solo-taught class with some help (i.e., the one teach/one support model). To ensure the intensity and the individualization of instruction needed by students with special needs, and to honor the IEP, co-teachers must incorporate all of the co-teaching models—one teach/one support; teaming; alternative; parallel; station—and focus on strategic instruction and monitor student progress.

Many students with special needs are taught using strategies that garner little success. Repeated use of inefficient strategies results in feelings of frustration, defeatist attitudes, and cycles of failure. Therefore, critical to the learning of students with special needs is the intentional introduction of specific strategies—those explicitly taught, practiced, and generalized to many occasions, and that support student attainment of IEP and curriculum goals—within the inclusive classroom.

Strategic learning is crucial to educational success, and effective strategies target the executive psychological functions that orchestrate learning and involve the processes of memory, attention, organization, mental shifting, impulse control, self-monitoring, planning and prioritizing, and task initiation (Meltzer, 2011). (For more information on executive functions, go to https://www.understood.org /en/learning-attention-issues/child-learning-disabilities

/executive-functioning-issues/key-executive-functioning-skills-explained; http://www.ldonline.org/article/24880/; https://www.verywell.com/executive-functioning-2162084; and https://www.verywell.com/what-are-executive-functions-20463.) Many of the learning deficiencies with which students with special needs struggle—reading, math, and writing skills—as well as test-taking, homework, and studying skills, involve difficulties with these critical executive functions (Meltzer & Krishnan, 2011). For example, organizing thoughts for writing paragraphs or essays, finding the important elements in a reading, holding on to sequences of sounds to form words, and sustained focused attention to specific tasks can be traced, in part, to executive functions.

In a co-taught inclusive setting, effective co-teachers co-plan to routinely explicitly teach and use strategies that pay off for students. Whether the strategy is in the form of specific steps to summarize and paraphrase, or a graphic story map to keep track of plot and character change, co-teachers must look at the curriculum expectations with IEP goals in mind. Co-teachers must also determine the effectiveness of the strategies they are teaching students to enable them to reach their IEP goals and achieve curriculum expectancies and keep, adjust, adapt, and change the strategies accordingly.

Answering the following questions can aid co-teachers as they devise strategies:

- What strategies are students using for particular tasks?
- How effectively do students use personal strategies?
- What strategies do we expect students to use for particular tasks?

- Are there strategies that we assume students already know and use (e.g., how to study for tests, how to remember information, how to organize a long-term project, how to answer multiple choice and essay questions)?
- What strategies do we actually teach?
- Which strategies will be the most useful? Used by students?
- How can we teach students to be strategic learners?
- How are students implementing the strategies we specifically teach?
- How are we supporting the generalization of strategies learned?

Parallel, station, and alternative co-teaching models are ideal for discussing, demonstrating, and practicing new strategies. Making the teaching and use of strategies routine decreases the amount of planning time needed. For any strategy to lead to academic success, it must be intentionally and explicitly taught through the following defined steps:

1. **Discussion**. Co-teachers and students discuss the complexity of the task and discover what strategies, if any, the students use.
2. **Self-Assessment**. Students assess the effectiveness and efficiency (or lack thereof) of the strategies they currently use.
3. **Rationale**. Co-teachers discuss with students the rationale for a new or adjusted strategy and how it will assist student learning and increase goal attainment.

4. **Modeling**. Co-teachers model the strategy.
5. **Guided practice**. Co-teachers guide students through the steps of the strategy.
6. **Peer practice**. Students practice the strategy in pairs.
7. **Independent practice**. Students implement the strategy on their own. (This step often requires some type of scaffolding until students are proficient in the strategy.)
8. **Generalization**. Co-teachers encourage and reinforce the use of the strategy in multiple contexts.
9. **Self-Monitoring**. Students use checklists to evaluate both their use of the strategy and their success.

Specific aspects of targeted strategy creation and instruction that make specific strategies more readily learned, remembered, and used (Hock, Deshler, & Schumaker, 2000) include:

- Delineation of the steps of the strategy that incorporate strategies students already know while weaving in elements to make the strategy more effective.
- Reworking, if possible, the steps so that each step begins with a verb, with the first letters of the first word of each step forming a mnemonic.
- Naming the strategy and writing specific steps on a strategy card.
- Using strategy cards to help students remember the strategy and reinforce correct use.

Strategies for Meeting IEP Goals

Elementary School Examples
IEP and Curriculum Goal: Find the main idea of readings.

Class strategy: Highlighting. The co-teachers taught the class to use colored highlighters as they read passages. Students are instructed to highlight important vocabulary in one color and key words and phrases in another color. Students are told to use yet another color to differentiate the main idea of the paragraphs.

Analysis of efficacy of strategy. The co-teachers analyzed students' highlighted passages. They realized that a large segment of students, including two with IEP goals to find the main idea of readings, appear to be using the highlighting strategy ineffectively: as they have difficulty differentiating between main ideas and details, much of the text is highlighted. As well, these students incorrectly answer questions associated with the readings.

Revised strategy. The co-teachers want to continue to use the highlighting strategy but realize that some of the students need to learn to target their highlighting. The co-teachers decide to employ the parallel co-teaching model when reading passages are assigned, with one co-teacher supervising the group of students who are successfully using the strategy, and the other co-teacher working closely with the group of students who need more targeted strategy instruction. The latter co-teacher discusses with the students the efficacy of their use of highlighting and the difficulties they are encountering and then incorporates an adapted version of the paraphrasing strategy (Deshler, Ellis & Lenz, 1996). Together, the co-teacher and the students devise a series of steps to find the main idea:

1. Number the paragraphs and read.
2. Use a blue highlighter to highlight who or what each paragraph is about.
3. Tell what's important about the who or the what in the paragraph by highlighting in green.
4. Summarize the reading by looking closely at the blue and green highlights.

The students call this finding the main idea strategy NUTS and create a strategy card with the steps. The NUTS strategy is modeled by the co-teacher, practiced, and generalized to all reading passages in all content areas.

Class strategy: Answering reading comprehension questions. The co-teachers taught the class to read test questions carefully and determine if the answers are on the line, between the lines, or a connection to something they already know.

Analysis of efficacy of strategy. The co-teachers analyzed student responses to questions on reading passages and determined that half the class is doing quite well and that the other half is performing inconsistently—with some performing quite poorly. They perform an error analysis of a few reading assessments and realize that errors are occurring on all types of questions and that even the students who seem to be doing well are making some mistakes.

Revised strategy. The co-teachers decide that the entire class could benefit from a more focused strategy. They begin by employing the station co-teaching model, with two teacher-led stations and one independent station. In one teacher-led station, the co-teacher reviews students' performance on reading comprehension assessments already taken. In the other teacher-led station, the co-teacher reads a passage with the students and they together answer the questions and discuss how to look at questions and answers. In the independent station, students are given a reading passage and the students have to match question cards with the correct answer cards. The students switch stations every 10 minutes.

The following day, employing the parallel co-teaching model, the co-teachers split the class into two heterogeneous groups. One co-teacher constructs with one group of students a strategy for answering questions while the other co-teacher leads the second group in a discussion on test-taking and what the students learned in the previous day's stations. After 20 minutes, the groups switch so each has discussion and strategy time.

The students, with their co-teacher, come up with a somewhat complicated strategy to answer comprehension questions:

1. **B**egin by closely reading the question and circling or underlining key words such as where, when, who, what, why, how.
2. **O**rganize your thoughts to see if you can answer the question before looking at the answers. If you can't, read the answers and put a check next to the one you think might be right.
3. **L**ook through the reading passage and underline or circle the parts that support your answer choice.
4. **T**ake some time, don't rush. If you are not positive, circle the question number and go on to the next question. Go back to the circled questions after all other questions are answered.
5. **S**top and then look over each question and your answer again. Put a + next to the answers you think you answered correctly.

The students put the steps of the BOLTS strategy on a strategy card and the co-teachers model the strategy and give students the opportunities to practice it and use it proficiently.

The co-teachers also put the NUTS & BOLTS strategies on laminated bookmarks and monitor use of the strategies by having students check off the steps as they perform them when reading passages and answering questions.

Secondary School Example

IEP and Curriculum Goal: Finding evidence from readings to support a position.

Class strategy: Annotations. Co-teachers instruct students to read actively and closely by writing key ideas and concepts, numbering steps and examples, inserting questions, making predictions, and summarizing in the margins of the readings.

Analysis of efficacy of strategy. Although many of the students write in the margins, the co-teachers wonder whether the notations are making a difference in student understanding of the texts. The writing is cramped and students don't seem to go back to the notes they make. Some students make very few notations.

Revised strategy. Co-teachers decide to simplify margin annotations for students. After discussing the strategy with students, using the parallel co-teaching model, one co-teacher introduces to a group of students annotation options that include using simple symbols to denote active reading: ✓ = understanding; ? = question; ! = surprise; * = important information; and + = new information. The students in this group are also instructed to use colored Post-its to represent opposition to the position (red Post-its) and support of the position (green Post-its). This co-teacher models and guides the use of these two strategies using passages from the novel the students are reading.

The other co-teacher introduces, models the use of, and guides the second group of students in their use of the Reading for Meaning organizer (Silver, Morris, & Klein, 2010), which is made up of three columns. The center column contains the position statement, the left column is for students' written evidence from the reading to support the statement, and the right column is for students' written evidence from the text that refutes the statement.

The co-teachers then switch groups so that all students in the class learn the three reading strategies.

Co-Planning Use of Technology for Accessible Learning

Using accessible instructional materials optimizes learning, and weaving technology into co-taught stations supports universal design for learning lessons and increases accessibility to learning. The straightforward principles of Universal Design for Learning (UDL) (see http://www.udlcenter.org/resource_library/articles)—of including multiple means of representation, expression, and engagement—benefit all learners in the inclusive classroom and advance learning for students with special needs. UDL is a flexible blueprint for developing curriculum that supports all learners through accessible tasks that are engaging and motivating, and that offers a variety of ways for teachers to represent information and for students to demonstrate understanding.

While technology is not synonymous with UDL, many lessons that incorporate UDL principles are more easily implemented through technology. In addition, the rising use of smartphones and personal computers in inclusive classes makes the attainment of higher standards more accessible for students with special needs. Lowering the barriers, not the bars, is a hallmark of UDL. The larger the achievement gap between students in an inclusive class, the more technology can be used to bridge the gap and provide for accessible learning materials for all (Hashey & Stahl, 2014). (For more information on technology and UDL and accessible educational materials, go to http://www.cast.org/search/Page+Type/aem_x003a_publicationdocument?page=1&query=aem; http://aem.cast.org/about#.VvmjCPkrKM8; and http://aem.cast.org/supporting/aem-learning.html#.Vx-tajArKM8.)

Text-to-Speech (TTS)

For example, Microsoft Windows Text-to-Speech, Google Text-to-Speech, No Visual Desktop Access, and Orca. This technology allows students to listen to text as it's displayed on the computer screen. Students with reading recognition deficits who are ordinarily unable to keep up with reading assignments can now "read" and reread print material by listening. TTS also assists students who understand print material if they can read and hear the text at the same time. TTS technology can be used by students in independent stations that require reading.

Interactive Whiteboards (IWBs)

For example, SMART board, Promethean. These are computer-connected, touch-sensitive displays that allow for a wide variety of presentations including videos, slideshows, and teacher and student interactions. An IWB in a co-taught classroom is commonly used for incorporating videos, presenting notes, demonstrating concepts, eliciting student responses, and interactively developing concepts and understandings. Limited research generally supports the educational benefits of IWBs (Marzano, 2009). This interactive technology, which commonly promotes whole class lessons, necessitates use of either the teaming or one teach/ one support co-teaching model. As much of the power of co-teaching is in focused teaching to small group, co-teachers need to think outside of the "interactive whiteboard box" to develop ways to use this technology in small group settings.

Learning Management Systems (LMSs) and Course Management Systems (CMSs)

For example, Blackboard, Moodle, Edmodo. These are online platforms that enable teachers and students to share material. Students have access to class notes, presentations, assignments, online quizzes, project calendars, links to websites, class readings, and e-mails. Customization of materials for individual students by co-teachers allows for targeted student support and monitoring of progress. Worksheets and grades can be posted and co-teachers can contact individual students directly, adapt projects, and establish record-keeping systems for goals.

L/CMSs are user friendly for teachers, students, and parents, all of whom can easily connect to an L/CMS via smartphones, tablets, and computers. Students can view calendars with due dates for assignments, review a list of assignments, communicate with co-teachers, and turn in assignments digitally. Audio embedded readings, digital flashcards for studying vocabulary, and virtual discussions between students and teachers provide limitless occasions for learning and feedback. Parental access to L/CMSs affords opportunities for tracking assignments, tests, and notes, and support of students. L/CMSs are a boon for co-teachers, enabling them to control course-work and access student work.

Google Apps for Education (GAfE)

For example, Google Docs, Sheets, Forms, and Slides. These provide co-teachers with a seamless means by which to collaborate on curriculum, presentations, and student worksheets. Co-teachers can remotely comment on, revise, and submit student assignments, learning packets, tests, and class presentations. Students can create documents and use them to collaborate with one another, perform peer reviews, and comment.

Video Editing Tools (VETs)

For example, Animoto, Screencast-O-Matic, ShowMe, Python, Screencastify. These tools enable co-teachers to capture class presentations, create animated cartoons, produce strategy videos, and develop online tutorials. The videos are often used by teachers employing the station co-teaching model or accessed by students for viewing at home. Students' access to videos from their homes allows for a flipped learning method through which students watch instructional videos for homework and work on practice assignments in class. Student viewing gives students the power to control their learning as they can review the videos repeatedly, take notes, and review material for upcoming tests or final exams.

Student Response Systems (SRSs)

For example, Pear Deck, Kahoot!, Mentimeter, SMART Response, Turning Technologies, Versal. These systems, sometimes called Bring Your Own Devise (BYOD), allow students to use their Internet-connected devices—smartphones or tablets—to immediately respond to co-teacher questions, polls, and quiz-embedded lessons. As students respond, co-teachers can assess levels of understanding and can quickly determine the need for re-teaching or extending concepts. Some SRSs are equipped with clickers, so students don't need their own devices. Others enable the insertion of images, videos, and text, and offer a variety of exercises that enable teachers to measure student learning and adapt instruction.

Which Technology Fits Best

In determining which technology would be most useful for instruction, co-teachers can consider the following questions:

- What forms of technology do we currently use to enhance the learning of our students?
- What technology with which we are familiar and are comfortable using might we incorporate more into our co-taught lessons?
- What technology is available within our classroom?
- What technology is available to our students outside of the classroom (library, home)?

- Where might we incorporate technology into some of our typical routines (e.g., review)?
- How does the technology we currently use provide access to understanding for our students?
- How does this technology provide opportunities for students with skill and conceptual deficits to advance?
- How does this technology change learning for students?
- How does this technology make learning more available to our students?
- How does this technology help lower the barriers to learning?
- How does this technology allow students to collaborate with peers?
- How does this technology encourage students to develop and showcase their individual strengths?
- If the technology doesn't work, what is our backup plan?

Technology in Action

Elementary School Examples

Instructional Videos. 4th grade co-teachers created a series of math instructional videos with ShowMe. Each four-minute video presented a distinct topic, such as *how to estimate* or *how to convert a decimal to a fraction*. The co-teachers, who employed the station model, routinely incorporated the videos in the independent stations. They paired the videos with review games, review sheets, and practice tests.

Editing Videos. 5th grade co-teachers used Screencastify to create personalized feedback on their students' writing. Students submitted their essays via Google Docs and the co-teachers captured the screens in video format and verbally communicated to the students what they needed to edit and how to revise the essays. Students used the verbal feedback to correct and expand their current work, and were also able to review the videos as they worked to achieve their writing goals.

Secondary School Examples

Video-Based Documents. Interactive intensive learning experiences through videos and questions based on videos is possible through Google Forms (Grotrain, 2015). Forms created by 9th grade Social Studies co-teachers included embedded videos with corresponding video-based questions. Students viewed the videos as many times as needed and answered the prompts relating to the videos. Responses were directly sent to the co-teachers' e-mail accounts, and individual responses and class summaries were generated. These co-teachers used this format for homework assignments and independent station activities.

Science Instructional Videos. Co-teachers of a 10th grade Earth Science class took turns creating 15-minute instructional videos for students to view at home. Each video focused on the presentation of a distinct element of the unit. They routinely assigned three videos a week. The videos freed up valuable class time. Upon entering the flipped classroom, students completed a short quiz on the previous night's topic to assess understanding of the material presented in the video. Students then went on to teacher-guided lab exercises during which the co-teachers reinforced the ideas and responded to students' knowledge based on the quiz.

Final Thoughts

Co-planning must be done routinely and strategically. Start slowly and realize that an effective co-taught class is significantly different than a solo-taught class. Start slowly and pick one predictable routine task or lesson and analyze all aspects of the routine and the effects on students. Start slowly and change some part of the co-taught lesson or routine to stimulate more effective learning. Look toward implementing a different co-teaching model, a revised strategy, or an accessible technology.

Pledge to use a co-teaching model that, though it may at first feel uncomfortable, will maximally benefit students. Use a co-teaching model that will facilitate a low student to teacher ratio—parallel or station—for a number of lessons. Reflect after each attempt, and commit to finding ways to make the model workable.

Pledge to look at the strategies taught and the strategies students use. Determine the effectiveness of the strategies and make changes (even slight ones) to make them more effective.

Pledge to incorporate into a routine technology that creates access to the level of knowledge students need to acquire. Commit to lowering barriers, not bars.

As different co-teaching models are implemented, new strategies are taught, and technology is incorporated into routines, thinking will slowly change during the co-planning of other lessons. Co-planning will become a pleasure and co-teachers will be amazed at how much more students are engaged and learn.

ENCORE

THE ROAD TO CO-PLANNING

Create a co-teaching team based on trust, hard work, reflection, and an openness to new ideas, and understand that a co-taught inclusive classroom is substantially different from a solo-taught classroom.

Organize teaching time by analyzing routines and incorporating powerful co-teaching models such as parallel and station.

Plan to scrutinize the efficacy of the strategies that you teach and that students use.

Look at technology as a way for students to access the complex components of learning.

Anticipate increased attainment of goals by students.

Notice that by varying the co-teaching models used, adjusting strategies, and incorporating technology into routines, student learning and knowledge is enhanced.

References

Deshler, D., Ellis, E., & Lenz, B. K. (1996). *Teaching adolescents with learning disabilities.* (2nd ed.) Denver, CO: Love Publishing Company.

Grotrain, K. (2015). *How to use video and Google Forms to encourage deeper learning.* Retrieved from http://www.eschoolnews.com/2015/10/20/video-google-deeper-713/.

Hashey, A., & Stahl, S. (2014). *Open educational resources: Designing for all learners.* Wakefield, MA: National Center on Accessing the General Curriculum. Retrieved from http://aem.cast.org/about/publications/2014/open-educational-resources-designing-all-learners.html.

Hock, M., Deshler, D., & Schumaker, J. (2000). *Strategic tutoring.* Lawrence, KS: Edge Enterprises.

Marzano, R. (2009). The art and science of teaching: Teaching with interactive whiteboards. *Educational Leadership, 67*(3), 80–82.

Meltzer, L. (Ed.). (2011). *Executive function in education: From theory to practice.* New York: Guilford Press.

Meltzer, L., & Krishnan, K. (2011). Executive function difficulties and learning disabilities: Understandings and misunderstandings. In Meltzer, L. (Ed.) *Executive function in education.* New York: Guilford Press.

Silver, H., Morris, S., & Klein, V. (2010). *Reading for meaning.* Alexandria, VA: ASCD.

Wilson, G.L. (2015). Revisiting classroom routines. *Educational Leadership, 73*(4), 50–55.

Wilson, G.L., & Blednick, J. (2011). *Teaching in tandem: Effective co-teaching in the inclusive classroom.* Alexandria, VA: ASCD.

Related Resources

At the time of publication, the following ASCD resources were available (ASCD stock numbers appear in parentheses). For up-to-date information about ASCD resources, go to www.ascd.org. You can search the complete archives of *Educational Leadership* at http://www.ascd.org/el.

ASCD Edge Group
Exchange ideas and connect with other educators interested in inclusion on the social networking site ASCDEdge® at http://ascdedge.ascd.org/.

Print Products
Educational Leadership: Co-Teaching: Making It Work (December 2015/January 2016) (#116031)

Educational Leadership: Multiple Measures: But What Kinds? (November 2009) (#110022)

Reading for Meaning: How to Build Students' Comprehension, Reasoning, and Problem-Solving Skills by Harvey F. Silver, Susan C. Morris, and Victor Klein (#110128)

Teaching in Tandem: Effective Co-Teaching in the Inclusive Classroom by Gloria Lodato Wilson and Joan Blednick (#110029)

For more information, send e-mail to member@ascd.org; call 1-800-933-2723 or 703-578-9600, press 2; send a fax to 703-575-5400; or write to Information Services, ASCD, 1703 N. Beauregard St., Alexandria, VA 22311-1714 USA.

About the Author

Gloria Lodato Wilson, PhD, is Professor of Special Education and Director of the graduate programs in secondary special education at Hofstra University. She collaborates with school districts to enhance their programs for students with special needs and English language learners by providing services to evaluate special education programs, giving workshops on effective teaching, progress monitoring, IEP development and Universal Design for Learning, and serving as a learning coach for co-teachers. Wilson, a former resource room and special education content teacher, taught children with multiple disabilities to swim, created and ran a preschool language clinic, taught students with autism in state and private schools, and created innovative programs for students with multiple disabilities in public schools. She received a National Teacher of the Year Award for her work in video therapy with students with special needs from NBC and the Carnegie Institute. Gloria's research interest is in the areas of teaching and learning strategies and effective co-teaching. She is the coauthor of *Teaching in Tandem: Effective Co-Teaching in the Inclusive Classroom*, and has scholarly articles in major special education journals.

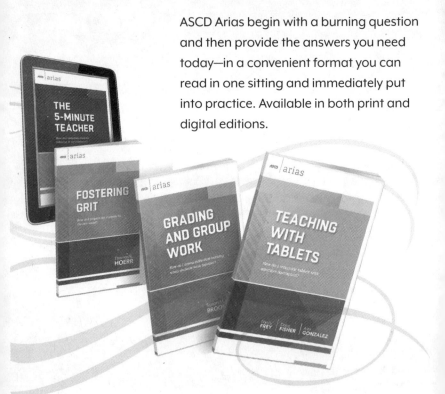